ICONS

SAFARI STYLE

SAFARI

Exteriors   Interiors

STYLE
Details

EDITOR **Angelika Taschen**

PHOTOS **Deidi von Schaewen**

TASCHEN

KÖLN LONDON LOS ANGELES MADRID PARIS TOKYO

Front cover: Two favourite places: on a verandah at Jao Camp, Botswana
Back cover: Hotel pet: at the Giraffe Manor hotel, near Nairobi

Couverture: Deux places de choix : sur la véranda du Jao Camp, Botswana
Dos de couverture: Animal domestique : à l'hôtel The Giraffe Manor, près de Nairobi

Umschlagvorderseite: Zwei Lieblingsplätze: Auf einer Veranda des Jao Camps, Botswana
Umschlagrückseite: Haustier: Im Hotel The Giraffe Manor, bei Nairobi

Also available from TASCHEN:

Inside Africa
2 Volumes, 912 pages
3–8228–5771–8

To stay informed about upcoming TASCHEN titles, please request our magazine at www.taschen.com or write to TASCHEN, Hohenzollernring 53, D-50672 Cologne, Germany, Fax: +49-221-254919. We will be happy to send you a free copy of our magazine which is filled with information about all of our books.

© 2004 TASCHEN GmbH
Hohenzollernring 53, D-50672 Köln
www.taschen.com

Concept by Angelika Taschen, Berlin
Layout and general project management by Stephanie Bischoff, Cologne
Texts by Christiane Reiter, Berlin
Lithography by Thomas Grell, Cologne
English Translation by Elaine Richards for First Edition Translations Ltd., Cambridge, England
French Translation by Thérèse Chatelain-Südkamp, Cologne

Printed in Italy
ISBN 3–8228–3852–7

CONTENTS SOMMAIRE INHALT

The air seemed like an oven, and a haze hung between us and the sky. The faded landscape resembled nothing so much as a Polaroid photograph whose colours have not quite come out properly. This Africa was no traditional beauty; it was much more than that: it was a dream. This was a land of unimagined vastness, with plains that rolled elegantly into the distance, dotted with trees whose sharply outlined shapes were like cut-out silhouettes. This was a realm of mountains that rose, menacing and unsettling, from the point where they merged imperceptibly into the green plains at their foot. It was a place of secrets, promising adventure and an encounter with a culture that could never be fully comprehended. Africa awakens the explorer in its visitors; they journey hour after hour through the bush in the hope of glimpsing the shadow of a leopard, herds of buffalo transforming a river into a foaming brown torrent, or elephants striding majestically toward their unknown destination. It is the excitement of the wild, of the unpredictable, and of danger that is the essence of these journeys of exploration – combined with the assurance of

SOMEWHERE IN AFRICA
Christiane Reiter

L'air avait la chaleur d'un four, le ciel semblait recouvert d'un léger voile et le paysage paraissait un peu pâle, comme sur une photo polaroïd dont les couleurs ne voudraient pas encore se révéler. Cette Afrique-là n'était pas d'une beauté classique, mais elle était bien plus, elle était un rêve. C'était un pays aux dimensions insoupçonnées, avec des espaces pleins d'élégance et des arbres dont la silhouette se découpait sur l'horizon. C'était le royaume des montagnes qui se dressaient menaçantes et apaisantes à la fois et qui, insensiblement, se métamorphosaient en une steppe verdoyante au bord du fleuve. C'était une région entourée de mystère, promettant l'aventure et la rencontre avec une culture qu'il est impossible de comprendre entièrement.
L'Afrique réveille le désir de la découverte qui sommeille chez ses visiteurs ; pendant des heures ils parcourent la brousse pour apercevoir l'ombre d'un léopard, admirer un troupeau de buffles qui transforment une rivière en un torrent impétueux ou guetter le passage des éléphants vers une destination inconnue. Le charme de telles expéditions, c'est cette vie sauvage, le danger, l'imprévu tout en sachant que l'on est en sécurité avec le ranger

Die Luft schien Backofentemperatur zu haben, vor dem Himmel hing ein zarter Schleier, und die Landschaft war ein bisschen blass – wie auf einem Polaroidfoto, das einfach nicht richtig bunt werden will. Eine klassische Schönheit war dieses Afrika nicht – aber es war viel mehr: Es war ein Traum. Ein Land von ungeahnten Ausmaßen, mit Ebenen, die elegant dahinflossen und Bäume besaßen, deren Silhouetten wie Scherenschnitte wirkten. Ein Reich der Berge, die bedrohend und beruhigend zugleich dastanden und am Fuß unmerklich in grüne Steppe übergingen. Eine Gegend voller Geheimnisse, die Abenteuer versprach und die Begegnung mit einer Kultur, die man niemals ganz verstehen würde. Afrika weckt die Entdecker in seinen Besuchern; sie sind stundenlang im Busch unterwegs, um den Schatten eines Leoparden zu erspähen, Büffelherden, die einen Fluss in braun schäumendes Wildwasser verwandeln, oder Elefanten, die majestätisch einem unbekannten Ziel entgegenziehen. Es ist der Reiz des Wilden, des Unberechenbaren und der Gefahr, der solche Erkundungstouren ausmacht – und zugleich das Wissen, in einer grundsätzlichen Sicherheit zu

security. They travel with a ranger who knows every inch of the ground, in a jeep whose four-wheel drive can cope with the most precarious situation, and there will be a camp able to conjure up English tea, a hot shower, and a four-poster bed in the midst of nowhere. "Safari lodge" may be a much-used marketing expression, but it captures the essential idea: a hotel or private house that invites guests to enter a different world of gnarled wood, rattan furniture, fabrics with exotic patterns, and fascinating art – all this with the creature comforts of home, even luxury. The lodges take care that no one gets lost in these unaccustomed realms. And here and there will be some amusing detail, a combination of the new and the familiar, such as a palm tree sketched out on the bathroom wall as if growing out of the cistern, a room divider of glass beads, or a curious giraffe peering in through the window. Discoveries like these are waiting to be made at the safari lodges on these pages – and almost all are available for bookings. Perhaps that is the best aspect of all: the dream of Africa can become a reality.

qui connaît chaque mètre carré du territoire, avec sa jeep capable de vous sortir de toutes les situations et avec le camp qui, au milieu de nulle part, vous permet de boire une tasse de thé, de prendre une douche chaude et de dormir dans un lit à baldaquin. Le « safari lodge », un terme devenu quelque peu rebattu, est pourtant une formule séduisante pour connaître l'Afrique. Un tel hôtel ou maison particulière transporte ses clients dans un autre univers avec ses bois noueux, ses meubles tressés, ses étoffes aux dessins exotiques et ses œuvres d'art fascinantes. Il permet de faire une pause tout en offrant le confort accoutumé ou même du grand luxe. On y trouve d'amusants détails comme un palmier dessiné sur le mur de la salle de bains, un paravent en perles de verre ou une girafe curieuse qui passe sa tête par la fenêtre. Les safari lodges présentés dans les pages suivantes vous invitent à de telles découvertes et le meilleur dans l'affaire, c'est qu'ils sont presque tous ouverts au public. Le rêve de l'Afrique peut ainsi devenir réalité.

leben. Denn da ist ein Ranger, der jeden Quadratmeter Boden kennt, ein Jeep, dessen Allradantrieb jeder brenzligen Situation zuvorkommt, oder ein Camp, das mitten im Nirgendwo englischen Tee, eine heiße Dusche und ein Himmelbett bietet. »Safari-Lodge« mag ein abgenutzter Marketingbegriff sein, doch er trifft den Kern der Sache: Ein solches Hotel oder Privathaus entführt seine Gäste in eine fremde Welt aus knorrigem Holz, geflochtenen Möbeln, Stoffen mit exotischen Mustern und faszinierender Kunst – und sorgt mit gewohntem Komfort oder sogar Luxus für Atempausen und dafür, dass in den neuen Sphären niemand verloren geht. Bisweilen sind es auch amüsante Details, die Altbekanntes und Neues verbinden: Eine an die Badezimmerwand gezeichnete Palme, die aus dem Wasserkasten »wächst«, ein Raumteiler aus glitzernden Glasperlen oder eine Giraffe, die neugierig ihren Kopf durchs Fenster streckt. Die Safari-Lodges auf den folgenden Seiten laden zu solchen Entdeckungen ein – und sind übrigens fast alle buchbar. Das ist vielleicht das Schönste daran: Der Traum von Afrika kann wahr werden.

"...The highland bush where the hunt takes place often looks like an abandoned garden in New England, until you climb a hill and realize that the garden is 50 miles long..."

Ernest Hemingway, in *49 Dispatches*

«...Le bush des hauts plateaux, où l'on va à la chasse, ressemble souvent à un jardin abandonné de la Nouvelle-Angleterre, jusqu'au moment où vous grimpez une montagne et réalis que le jardin est long de 80 kilomètres...»

Ernest Hemingway, dans *49 dépêches*

»...Der Hochlandbusch, wo man auf die Jagd geht, sieht oft wie ein verlassener Garten in New England aus, bis Sie einen Berg besteigen und merken, dass der Garten 80 Kilometer lang ist...»

Ernest Hemingway, in *49 Depeschen*

EXTERIORS

Extérieurs   Aussichten

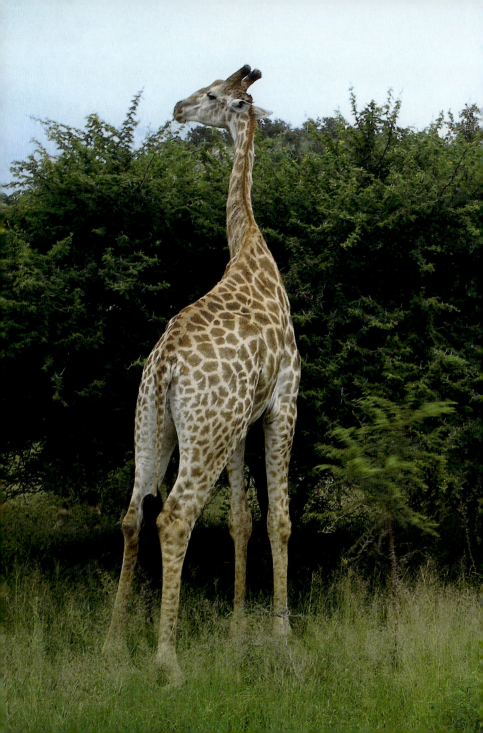

10/11 Built by the water: bungalows of Mombo Camp, Botswana. *Construits au bord de l'eau : bungalows du Mombo Camp, Botswana.* Nahe am Wasser gebaut: Bungalows des Mombo Camps, Botswana.

12/13 Lighting the way: in Makalali Private Game Reserve, South Africa. *Chemin éclairé : dans la réserve Makalali Private Game, Afrique du Sud.* Den Weg leuchten: Im Makalali Private Game Reserve, Südafrika.

14/15 Just as nature left it: gnarled tree trunks in Makalali Private Game Reserve. *Laissés à l'état naturel : troncs noueux dans la réserve Makalali Private Game.* Naturbelassen: Knorrige Stämme im Makalali Private Game Reserve.

16/17 A gentle breeze: on Anna Trzebinski's balcony, Nairobi. *Légère brise : sur le balcon d'Anna Trzebinski, Nairobi.* Leichte Brise: Auf dem Balkon von Anna Trzebinski, Nairobi.

18/19 Reflections: Alan Donovan's pool and bathing pavilion, Nairobi. *Effet de miroir : la piscine et le pavillon de bains d'Alan Donovan, Nairobi.* Spiegelbild: Pool und Badepavillon von Alan Donovan, Nairobi.

20/21 Million-dollar view: from Ngorongoro Crater Lodge, Tanzania. *Une vue valant un million de dollars : depuis le Ngorongoro Crater Lodge, Tanzanie.* Der Million-Dollar-Blick: Von der Ngorongoro Crater Lodge aus gesehen, Tansania.

22/23 Grey giants: elephants in Ngorongoro Conservation Area, Tanzania. *Géants gris : éléphants dans la Ngorongoro Conservation Area, Tanzanie.* Graue Giganten: Elefanten in der Ngorongoro Conservation Area, Tansania.

24/25 Herd instinct: buffaloes in Ngorongoro Conservation Area. *Instinct grégaire : buffles dans la Ngorongoro Conservation Area.* Herdentrieb: Büffel in der Ngorongoro Conservation Area.

26/27 Bush art: in Makalali Private Game Reserve, South Africa. *Bush artistique : dans la réserve Makalali Private Game, Afrique du Sud.* Kunst am Busch: Im Makalali Private Game Reserve, Südafrika.

28/29 Tucked away: hidden bungalow in Makalali Private Game Reserve. *Caché dans la nature : bungalow dans la réserve Makalali Private Game.* Eingewachsen: Versteckter Bungalow im Makalali Private Game Reserve.

30/31 Picnic by the river: near Makalali Private Game Reserve. *Pique-nique au bord du fleuve : dans les environs de la réserve Makalali Private Game .* Picknick am Fluss: In der Nähe des Makalali Private Game Reserves.

32/33 Green giant: huge tree in Mombo Camp, Botswana. *Grand et verdoyant : arbre imposant au Mombo Camp, Botswana.* Groß und grün: Mächtiger Baum im Mombo Camp, Botswana.

34/35 All-round heat: a fireplace in Mombo Camp. *Rondement mené : un feu au Mombo Camp.* Runde Sache: Eine Feuerstelle im Mombo Camp.

36/37 Feeding time: in front of the Giraffe Manor hotel, near Nairobi. *L'heure de la nourriture : devant l'hôtel The Giraffe Manor, près de Nairobi.* Fütterungszeit: Vor dem Hotel The Giraffe Manor, bei Nairobi.

38/39 Tea for two: at the colourfully decorated table in the garden of Dodo's Tower, Kenya. *Tea for two : table colorée dans le jardin de Dodo's Tower, Kenya.* Tea for two: Am bunt geschmückten Tisch im Garten von Dodo's Tower, Kenia.

40/41 Inviting: somewhere to relax at Lake Naivasha, Kenya. *Invitation au repos : près du lac de Naivasha, Kenya.* Zum Hineinlegen schön: Ruheplätze am Naivashasee, Kenia.

42/43 Round pavilion: in the garden surrounding Dodo's Tower. *Pavillon rond : dans le jardin autour de Dodo's Tower.* Runder Pavillon: Im Garten rund um Dodo's Tower.

44/45 Head in the clouds: two giraffes, with Dodo's Tower in the background. *Dans les sphères supérieures: deux girafes et au fond Dodo's Tower.* In höheren Sphären: Zwei Giraffen und im Hintergrund Dodo's Tower.

46/47 Breakfast with a view: in Ngorongoro Crater Lodge, Tanzania. *Un petit-déjeuner avec vue : dans le Ngorongoro Crater Lodge, Tanzanie.* Frühstück mit Aussicht: In der Ngorongoro Crater Lodge, Tansania.

48/49 Perfect pattern: giraffes and zebras at Jao Camp, Botswana. *Taches et rayures : girafes et zèbres près du Jao Camp, Botswana.* Mustergültig: Giraffen und Zebras beim Jao Camp, Botswana.

50/51 Stalking: leopard near Jao Camp, Botswana. *A la recherche d'une proie : léopard près du Jao Camp, Botswana.* Auf der Pirsch: Leopard nahe des Jao Camps, Botswana.

52/53 On stilts: restaurant and lounge terrace of Mombo Camp, Botswana. *Sur pilotis : terrasse du restaurant et du lounge au Mombo Camp, Botswana.* Auf Stelzen: Restaurant- und Loungeterrasse des Mombo Camps, Botswana.

54/55 Put your feet up: chill out in Mombo Camp. *Relax : chill out au Mombo Camp.* Einfach die Füße hoch legen: Chill out im Mombo Camp.

56/57 Beautiful blue: plunge pool in Mombo Camp. *Bleu vif : petite piscine privée au Mombo Camp .* Leuchtend blau: Kleiner Privatpool im Mombo Camp.

58/59 The tastiest leaves are at the top: giraffes looking for food. *Tout en haut les feuilles sont les plus tendres : girafes cherchant de la nourriture.* Ganz oben sind die Blätter am zartesten: Giraffen auf Nahrungssuche.

60/61 Where dreams come true: relaxation area in Mombo Camp. *Là où les rêves deviennent réalité : un pavillon de repos au Mombo Camp.* Wo Träume wahr werden: Ein Ruhepavillon im Mombo Camp.

62/63 Framed in teak: the pool of Makalali Private Game Reserve. *Cerclée de bois de teck : la piscine de la réserve Makalali Private Game .* Mit Teakholz eingefasst: Der Pool des *Makalali Private Game Reserves.*

64/65 In the gloaming: open-air restaurant around the camp fire at Mombo Camp. *Heure bleue : restaurant en plein air autour du feu de camp au Mombo Camp.* Blaue Stunde: Open-Air-Restaurant rund ums Lagerfeuer im Mombo Camp.

"…Sandalwood makes the air smell sweet, birds trill in their cages about peace and solitude and the cool of the rainforest…"

Thomas Corghessan Boyle, in *Water music*

«…Le bois de santal donne à l'air un parfum suave, dans leurs cages les oiseaux chantent la paix et la solitude, la fraîcheur de la forêt tropicale…»

Thomas Corghessan Boyle , dans *Water Music*

»…Sandelholz lässt die Luft süßlich duften, in Käfigen trällern Vögel von Frieden und Einsamkeit, von der Kühle des Regenwalds…«

Thomas Corghessan Boyle, in: *Wassermusik*

INTERIORS

Intérieurs Einsichten

72/73 Like earthborne fluffy clouds: sofas in Mnemba Island Lodge, near Zanzibar. *Comme des nuages sur terre : sofas dans le Mnemba Island Lodge, près de Zanzibar.* Wie Wattewolken auf der Erde: Sofas in der Mnemba Island Lodge, bei Sansibar.

74/75 Artistic flooring: in Chumbe Island Coral Park, near Zanzibar. *Sol artistique : au Chumbe Island Coral Park, près de Zanzibar.* Kunstvoller Fußboden: Im Chumbe Island Coral Park, bei Sansibar.

76/77 Tenderly entwined: sheltered bed in Chumbe Island Coral Park. *Doux filets : lit protégé au Chumbe Island Coral Park.* Zarte Netze: Geschütztes Bett im Chumbe Island Coral Park.

78/79 Wood and stone. Staircase at Jao Camp, Botswana. *En bois et en pierre : escalier au Jao Camp, Botswana.* Aus Holz und Stein: Treppenhaus des Jao Camps, Botswana.

80/81 Mixture of materials: lounge in Mombo Camp, Botswana. *Mélange de matériaux : lounge au Mombo Camp, Botswana.* Materialmix: Lounge im Mombo Camp, Botswana.

82/83 Shades of brown and beige: seating group in Mombo Camp. *Dans des tons de brun et de beige : groupe de sièges au Mombo Camp.* In Braun- und Beigetönen: Sitzgruppe im Mombo Camp.

84/85 Brightly coloured cushions: in the separate guestroom of Anna Trzebinski, Nairobi. *Coussins colorés : dans la chambre d' hôtes séparee d'Anna Trzebinski, Nairobi.* Bunte Kissen: Im separaten Gästezimmer von Anna Trzebinski, Nairobi.

86/87 Enthroned in the library: an airy room in Mombo Camp. *Trôner dans la bibliothèque : pièce aérée au Mombo Camp.* In der Bibliothek thronen: Luftiger Raum im Mombo Camp.

88/89 Beneath high ceilings: relaxing at Mombo Camp. *Sous des plafonds hauts : se détendre au Mombo Camp.* Unter hohen Decken: Entspannen im Mombo Camp.

90/91 Playing shadows: sheltered sitting area at Mombo Camp. *Jeux d'ombre : coin protégé au Mombo Camp.* Schattenspiele: Geschützter Sitzbereich im Mombo Camp.

92/93 Long tables for long evenings: a dining table in Mombo Camp. *Longue table pour une longue soirée : table au Mombo Camp.* Lange Tafel für lange Abende: Esstisch im Mombo Camp.

94/95 Seventh heaven: bed of Anna Trzebinski, Nairobi. *Au septième ciel : le lit d'Anna Trzebinski, Nairobi.* Wie auf Wolke sieben: Das Bett von Anna Trzebinski, Nairobi.

96/97 In true British style: library in the Giraffe Manor hotel, near Nairobi. *Très british : la bibliothèque à l'hôtel The Giraffe Manor, près de Nairobi.* Auf die britische Art: Bibliothek im Hotel The Giraffe Manor, bei Nairobi.

98/99 Profusely patterned: bedroom in Hippo Point House, Kenya. *Des motifs à foison : chambre au Hippo Point House, Kenya.* Üppig gemustert: Schlafzimmer im Hippo Point House, Kenia.

100/101 Wall painting: designs from nature in the bathroom of Hippo Point House. *Peinture murale : tableaux naturels dans la salle de bains de Hippo Point House.* Wandmalerei: Naturbilder im Bad des Hippo Point Houses.

102/103 Colonial flair: in the private living room of Armando Tanzini, Kenya. *Ambiance coloniale : dans le salon privé d'Armando Tanzini, Kenya.* Koloniales Flair: Im privaten Salon von Armando Tanzini, Kenia.

104/105 Showpiece: magnificent door frame in Armando Tanzini's house. *Véritable joyau : somptueux cadre de porte dans la maison d'Armando Tanzini.* Schmuckstück: Prachtvoller Türrahmen im Haus von Armando Tanzini.

106/107 Swathed in silk: Armando Tanzini's four-poster bed. *Recouvert de soie : le lit à baldaquin d'Armando Tanzini.* Mit Seide umhüllt: Das Himmelbett von Armando Tanzini.

108/109 Dinner is served: dining room at Ngorongoro Crater Lodge, Tanzania. *Le dîner est prêt : salle à manger au Ngorongoro Crater Lodge, Tanzanie.* Es ist angerichtet: Esszimmer in der Ngorongoro Crater Lodge, Tansania.

110/111 Massive hearthside furnishings: sitting room of Ngorongoro Crater Lodge. *Meubles imposants près de la cheminée : le salon du Ngorongoro Crater Lodge.* Mächtiges Mobiliar am Kamin: Salon der Ngorongoro Crater Lodge.

112/113 Africa meets Asia: the brown sitting room of Jao Camp, Botswana. *Africa meets Asia : dans le salon marron du Jao Camp, Botswana.* Africa meets Asia: Im braunen Salon des Jao Camps, Botswana.

114/115 Highlight of craftwork: a bright suite in Jao Camp. *Artisanat d'art : une suite claire au Jao Camp.* Kunsthandwerk setzt Akzente: Eine helle Suite im Jao Camp.

116/117 Washing facilities: an unusual bathroom with a chaise longue in Jao Camp. *Pour les ablutions : salle de bains hors du commun avec chaise longue au Jao Camp.* Waschgelegenheit: Außergewöhnliches Badezimmer mit Ruheliege im Jao Camp.

118/119 Camping de luxe: golden light at Mombo Camp, Botswana. *Tentes de luxe : lumière dorée au Mombo Camp, Botswana.* Zelten de luxe: Goldenes Licht im Mombo Camp, Botswana.

120/121   The zebra look: Singita Boulders
Lodge, South Africa. *Look zèbre : au Singita
Boulders Lodge, Afrique du Sud.* Im Zebra-
look: In der Singita Boulders Lodge, Südafrika.

122/123   A splash of colour: the living room at
Makalali Private Game Reserve. *Taches de
couleur : dans la salle de séjour de la réserve
Makalali Private Game.* Farbtupfer: Im Wohn-
zimmer des Makalali Private Game Reserves.

124/125   Brightly patterned: bed with bed-
hangings at Makalali Private Game Reserve.
*Motif coloré : lit à baldaquin de la réserve
Makalali Private Game.* Bunte Muster: Über-
dachtes Bett im Makalali Private Game Reserve.

126/127   Open-air bathing: artistically decorat-
ed bathtub at Makalali Private Game Reserve.
*Salle de bains en plein air : baignoire artiste-
ment décorée de la réserve Makalali Private
Game.* Open-air-Bad: Kunstvoll verzierte
Wanne im Makalali Private Game Reserve.

"…You remember the curve of a wheeltrack in the grass of the plain as if it had imprinted itself on your mind…"

Tania Blixen, in *Out of Africa*

«…On se souvient de la courbe d'une trace de roue dans l'herbe de la plaine comme si elle s'était imprimée dans notre esprit…»

Tania Blixen , dans *La ferme africaine*

»…Man erinnert sich an die Kurve einer Radspur im Gras der Steppe, als hätte sie sich einem ins Gemüt gedrückt…«

Tania Blixen, in *Jenseits von Afrika*

DETAILS

Détails Details

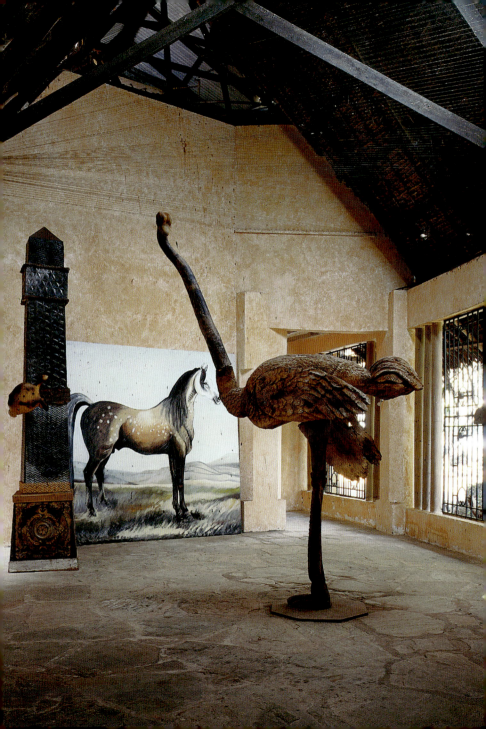

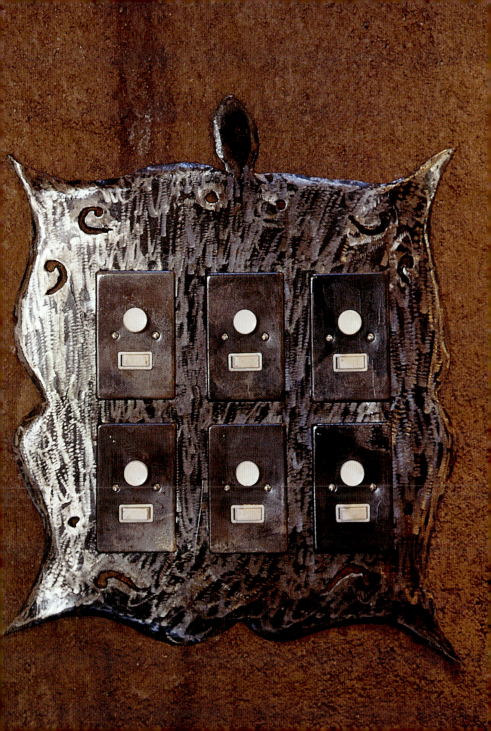

134 Homage to Masai art: a room in the Kitengela glass factory, Kenya. *Hommage à l'art des Massaï : pièce dans la verrerie Kitengela, Kenya.* Hommage an die Kunst der Massai: Raum in der Glasfabrik Kitengela, Kenia.

136 Trophies: three animal skulls in the Kitengela glass factory. *Trophées : trois crânes d'animaux dans la verrerie Kitengela.* Trophäen: Drei Tierschädel in der Glasfabrik Kitengela.

137 The man in the moon: mask from Burkina Faso at Alan Donovan's house, Kenya. *Homme lunaire : masque du Burkina Faso chez Alan Donovan, Kenya.* Vom Mann im Mond: Maske aus Burkina Faso bei Alan Donovan, Kenia.

138 Shades of brown: fabrics from the Congo in Alan Donovan's house. *Tons de brun : étoffe du Congo dans la maison d'Alan Donovan.* In Brauntönen: Stoffe aus dem Kongo im Haus von Alan Donovan.

140 Art of the natural: in Armando Tanzini's house, Kenya. *Naturelle et artificielle : la maison d'Armando Tanzini, Kenya.* Natürlich künstlich: Im Haus von Armando Tanzini, Kenia.

141 Beneath the palm trees: in Hippo Point House, Kenya. *Sous les palmiers : dans la Hippo Point House, Kenya.* Platz unter Palmen: In Hippo Point House, Kenia.

142 Hideaway for water nymphs: bath in Ngorongoro Crater Lodge, Tanzania. *Refuge pour les nixes : salle de bains au Ngorongoro Crater Lodge, Tanzanie.* Nische für Nixen: Bad in der Ngorongoro Crater Lodge, Tansania.

144 Elegance of form: Carafes from Kitengela. *Beauté des formes : carafes de Kitengela.* Formschön: Karaffen aus Kitengela.

145 Exotic: "mkadi" fruit from Tanzania. *Exotique : le fruit « mkadi » de Tanzanie.* Exotisch: Die Frucht »Mkadi« aus Tansania.

146 Glass bead curtain: a shower curtain at Mnemba Island Lodge, off Zanzibar. *En perles de verre : rideau de douche au Mnemba Island Lodge, près de Zanzibar.* Aus Glasperlen: Duschvorhang in der Mnemba Island Lodge, bei Sansibar.

148 Strung strands: a curtain of small stones in Mombo Camp, Botswana. *Enfilées une à une : rideau de petites pierres au Mombo Camp, Botswana.* Aufgefädelt: Vorhang aus kleinen Steinen im Mombo Camp, Botswana.

149 Just curious: in the Giraffe Manor hotel, near Nairobi. *Curieuse : à l'hôtel The Giraffe Manor, près de Nairobi.* Neugierig: Im Hotel The Giraffe Manor, bei Nairobi.

150 Touching wood: massive door in Jao Camp, Botswana. *Touchez du bois : porte imposante au Jao Camp, Botswana.* Auf Holz klopfen: Mächtige Tür im Jao Camp, Botswana.

152 Washstand: in Mombo Camp, Botswana. *Lavabo : au Mombo Camp, Botswana.* Waschtisch: Im Mombo Camp, Botswana.

153 Bathing beneath the trees: open-air shower in Mombo Camp. *Salle de bains sous les arbres : douche en plein air au Mombo Camp.* Bad unter Bäumen: Freiluft-dusche im Mombo Camp.

154 Decorative seats: in Jao Camp, Botswana. *Petits bijoux : sièges au Jao Camp, Botswana.* Schmuckvolle Sitze: Im Jao Camp, Botswana.

156 Water from above: open-air shower in Jao Camp. *Une ondée agréable : douche en plein air au Jao Camp.* Wasser von oben: Open-Air-Dusche im Jao Camp.

157 Beautiful curves: door handles in Singita Boulders Lodge. *Joliment recourbées : poignées de porte au Singita Boulders Lodge.* Schön geschwungen: Tür-griffe in der Singita Boulders Lodge.

158 Neat circle: fireplace in Jao Camp, Botswana. *Rondelle : un feu au Jao Camp, Botswana.* Rondell: Feuerstelle im Jao Camp, Botswana.

160 Behind bars: crockery cupboard in Hippo Point House, Kenya. *Grillagé : vaisselier au Hippo Point House, Kenya.* Hinter Gittern: Geschirrschrank im Hippo Point House, Kenia.

161 Animal at the door: at Makalali Private Game Reserve. *Animal à la porte : de la réserve Makalali Private Game.* Tier an der Tür: im Makalali Private Game Reserve.

162 Gem: portable bar in Dodo's Tower, Kenya. *Bijou : bar portable au Dodo's Tower, Kenya.* Klein-od: Portable Bar in Dodo's Tower, Kenia.

164 In the style of ancient art: animal sketches. *D'après un art millénaire : dessins d'animaux.* Nach alter Kunst: Tierzeichnungen.

165 Generously framed: decoration in Makalali Private Game Reserve. *Cadre épais : décora-tion dans la réserve Makalali Private Game.* Dick einge-rahmt: Dekoration im Makalali Private Game Reserve.

166 Well uphol-stered: covered hall-way in Mnemba Island Lodge. *Bien capitonné : couloir couvert au Mnemba Island Lodge.* Gut gepolstert: Über-dachter Flur in der Mnemba Island Lodge.

168 Organically shaped vases: at Alan Donovan's house, Nairobi. *Vases aux formes organiques : chez Alan Donovan, Nairobi.* Organisch geformte Vasen: Bei Alan Donovan, Nairobi.

169 Step by step: staircase in Jao Camp, Botswana. *Pour les allées et venues : escalier au Jao Camp, Botswana.* Auf Schritt und Tritt: Treppe im Jao Camp, Botswana.

170 Tables cleared: kitchen in a private lodge, South Africa. *Bien rangée : cuisine dans la lodge privée, Afrique du Sud.* Aufgeräumt: Küche in einer privaten Lodge, Südafrika.

172 In the heart of nature: narrow path in Jao Camp, Botswana. *A travers la nature : petit sentier au Jao Camp, Botswana.* Mitten durch die Natur: Schmaler Weg im Jao Camp, Botswana.

173 Bathing under the greenwood tree: an outdoor shower in Jao Camp. *Baignade dans la verdure : douche en plein air au Jao Camp.* Baden im Grünen: Außendusche im Jao Camp.

174 Blue bathroom: toilet in Mombo Camp, Botswana. *Salle de bains bleue : toilettes au Mombo Camp, Botswana.* Bad in Blau: Toilette im Mombo Camp, Botswana.

176 No slatted frame this: woven bed in Mombo Camp. *En guise de sommier: couche tressée au Mombo Camp.* Statt Lattenrost: Geflochtene Liegefläche im Mombo Camp.

177 Chessboard pattern: wooden steps at Mombo Camp. *Motif d'échiquier : marches en bois au Mombo Camp.* Schachbrettmuster: Hölzerne Stufen im Mombo Camp.

178 Proceedings suspended: daybed in Ngorongoro Crater Lodge, Tanzania. *Semble flotter : lit de repos au Ngorongoro Crater Lodge, Tanzanie.* Schwebendes Verfahren: Tagesbett in der Ngorongoro Crater Lodge, Tansania.

180 Double curtains: windows in the Blue Safari Club, Kenya. *Rideaux doubles : fenêtre au Blue Safari Club, Kenya.* Doppelte Vorhänge: Fenster im Blue Safari Club, Kenia.

181 The best seats: easy chairs in the Blue Safari Club, Kenya. *Places avec vue : fauteuils confortables au Blue Safari Club, Kenya.* Aussichtsplätze: Bequeme Sessel im Blue Safari Club, Kenia.

182 Gaily decorated: glasses and carafes. *Multicolores : verres et carafes.* Bunt verziert: Gläser und Karaffen.

184 Vitamin-rich: a snack of dried fruit. *Riche en vitamines : fruits secs en en-cas.* Vitaminreich: Getrocknetes Obst als Snack.

185 Sextet: in a private lodge, South Africa. *Sextuor : dans la lodge privée, Afrique du Sud.* Sextett: In einer privaten Lodge, Südafrika.

186 At ease: elephant near Ngorongoro Crater Lodge, Tanzania. *Paisible : éléphant près du Ngorongoro Crater Lodge, Tanzanie.* Ganz gelassen: Elefant nahe der Ngorongoro Crater Lodge, Tansania.

Addresses

BLUE SAFARI CLUB
P.O. Box 15026
00509 Langata
Nairobi, Kenya
Tel. (254) 20 890184, Fax 890096
E-mail: info@bluesafariclub.com
Website: www.bluesafariclub.com

DODO'S TOWER
P.O. Box 24397
Nairobi, Kenya
Tel. (254) 20 574689, Fax 577381
E-mail: mellifera@swiftkenya.com

ALAN DONOVAN
P.O. Box l7871
Nairobi, Kenya
Tel. & Fax. (254) 45 22476
E-mail: ahalan@africaonline.co.ke

THE GIRAFFE MANOR
P.O. Box 15004
Langata, Nairobi, Kenya
Tel. (254) 20 891078, Fax 890949
E-mail: giraffem@kenyaweb.com
Website: www.giraffemanor.com

HIPPO POINT HOUSE
P.O. Box 1852
Naivasha, Kenya
Tel. (254) 311 30124, Fax 20098
E-mail: hippo-pt@africaonline.co.ke
Website: www.hippo-pointkenya.com

CHUMBE ISLAND CORAL PARK
P.O. Box 3203
Zanzibar, Tanzania
Tel. & Fax. (255) 24 2231040
E-mail: info@chumbeisland.com
Website: www.chumbeisland.com

MNEMBA ISLAND LODGE
P.O. Box 2055
Zanzibar, Tanzania
Tel. (255) 24 2233110, Fax 2233117
E-mail: webenquiries@ccafrica.com
Website: www.mnemba-island.com

NGORONGORO CRATER LODGE
Ngorongoro Conservation Area
Tanzania
Tel. (255) 27 2537038, Fax 2548296
E-mail: information@ccafrica.com
Website: www.ccafrica.com

JAO CAMP
Okavango Delta, Botswana
Tel. (27) 11 8071800, Fax 8072100
E-mail: enquiry@wilderness.co.za
Website: www.wilderness-safaris.com

MOMBO CAMP
Moremi Game Reserve
Okavango Delta, Botswana
Tel. (27) 11 8071800, Fax 8072100
E-mail: enquiry@wilderness.co.za
Website: www.wilderness-safaris.com

SINGITA BOULDERS LODGE
Sabi Sand Game Reserve
Krüger Nationalpark, Province Mpumalanga
South Africa
Tel. (27) 13 7355456, Fax 7355746
E-mail: reservartions@singita.co.za
Website: www.singita.com

GARONGA LODGE
P.O. Box 737
Hoedspruit 1380
Province Limpopo
South Africa
Tel. (27) 11 5374620, Fax 4470993
E-mail: reservations@garonga.com
Website: www.garonga.com

MAKALALI PRIVATE GAME RESERVE
P.O. Box 809
Hoedspruit 1380
Province Limpopo
South Africa
Tel. (27) 15 7931720, Fax 7931739
E-mail: makalali@mweb.co.za
Website: www.makalali.com

Architect

Mombo Camp, Makalali Private Game Reserve,
Jao Camp and Ngorongoro Crater Lodge were
designed by the architect Silvio Rech, South Africa
E-mail: adventarch@mweb.co.za

The Hotel Book.
Great Escapes Africa
Ed. Angelika Taschen / Shelley-Maree
Cassidy / Hardcover, 400 pp. /
€ 29.99 / $ 39.99 / £ 19.99 /
¥ 5.900

Inside Africa
Ed. Angelika Taschen / Deidi von
Schaewen / Hardcover, 2 volumes,
912 pp. / € 99.99 / $ 125 /
£ 69.99 / ¥ 15.000

"In two volumes, this is a remarkable, colossal undertaking – more than simply a visual source book." —*House & Garden,* London, on *Inside Africa*

"Buy them all and add some pleasure to your life."

All-American Ads 40s
Ed. Jim Heimann

All-American Ads 50s
Ed. Jim Heimann

All-American Ads 60s
Ed. Jim Heimann

Angels
Gilles Néret

Architecture Now!
Ed. Philip Jodidio

Art Now
Eds. Burkhard Riemschneider,
Uta Grosenick

Berlin Style
Ed. Angelika Taschen

Chairs
Charlotte & Peter Fiell

Design of the 20th Century
Charlotte & Peter Fiell

Design for the 21st Century
Charlotte & Peter Fiell

Devils
Gilles Néret

Digital Beauties
Ed. Julius Wiedemann

Robert Doisneau
Ed. Jean-Claude Gautrand

East German Design
Ralf Ulrich / Photos: Ernst
Hedler

Eccentric Style
Ed. Angelika Taschen

Fashion
Ed. The Kyoto Costume
Institute

HR Giger
HR Giger

Graphic Design
Ed. Charlotte & Peter Fiell

Grand Tour
Harry Seidler,
Ed. Peter Gössel

Havana Style
Ed. Angelika Taschen

Homo Art
Gilles Néret

Hot Rods
Ed. Coco Shinomiya

Hula
Ed. Jim Heimann

India Bazaar
Samantha Harrison,
Bari Kumar

Industrial Design
Charlotte & Peter Fiell

Japanese Beauties
Ed. Alex Gross

Kitchen Kitsch
Ed. Jim Heimann

Krazy Kids' Food
Eds. Steve Roden,
Dan Goodsell

Las Vegas
Ed. Jim Heimann

Mexicana
Ed. Jim Heimann

Morocco Style
Ed. Angelika Taschen

**Extra/Ordinary Objects,
Vol. I**
Ed. Colors Magazine

**Extra/Ordinary Objects,
Vol. II**
Ed. Colors Magazine

Paris Style
Ed. Angelika Taschen

Penguin
Frans Lanting

Photo Icons, Vol. I
Hans-Michael Koetzle

Photo Icons, Vol. II
Hans-Michael Koetzle

20th Century Photography
Museum Ludwig Cologne

Pin-Ups
Ed. Burkhard Riemschneider

Provence Style
Ed. Angelika Taschen

Pussycats
Gilles Néret

Safari Style
Ed. Angelika Taschen

Seaside Style
Ed. Angelika Taschen

Albertus Seba. Butterflies
Irmgard Müsch

**Albertus Seba. Shells &
Corals**
Irmgard Müsch

Starck
Ed Mae Cooper, Pierre Doze,
Elisabeth Laville

Surfing
Ed. Jim Heimann

Sydney Style
Ed. Angelika Taschen

Tattoos
Ed. Henk Schiffmacher

Tiffany
Jacob Baal-Teshuva

Tiki Style
Sven Kirsten

Tuscany Style
Ed. Angelika Taschen

Women Artists
in the 20th and 21st Century
Ed. Uta Grosenick

ICONS